IMAGES
of America

NEW HAVEN
FROM THE COLLECTION OF
CHARLES RUFUS HARTE

IMAGES
of America

NEW HAVEN
FROM THE COLLECTION OF
CHARLES RUFUS HARTE

By
Frederick W. Chesson

ARCADIA

First published 1995
Copyright © Frederick W. Chesson, 1995

ISBN 0-7524-0212-9

Published by Arcadia Publishing,
an imprint of the Chalford Publishing Corporation
One Washington Center, Dover, New Hampshire 03820
Printed in Great Britain

Library of Congress Cataloging-in-Publication Data applied for

To Charles Rufus Harte (1870–1956) a true Rennaissance Man of
the late nineteenth and mid-twentieth centuries, whose times
spanned from the Reconstruction Era to the Space Age, this
book is gratefully and fondly dedicated.

Also in memory of John Williams Harte
and Rebekah Harte Clarke.

Contents

Harkness Tower, photographed in June 1940.

Foreword

This publication, to say nothing of the preservation of a treasury of historical photographs, could not have come about had it not been for a certain specialized parallel interest between Charles Rufus Harte and myself: Roxbury, Connecticut's unique Mine Hill.

In April and May of 1934, as part of his study of Connecticut's vanished iron industry, Harte visited historic Mine Hill, rising above Roxbury Station on the Shepaug River. He took about fifty photographs, some of the soon-to-vanish blast furnace structures and even of a resident bat in one of the dank tunnels. He then went on to document the more extensive relics in the northwest corner, especially in the Canaan-Salisbury area.

After taking hundreds of pictures of crumbling furnaces stacks, rotting water wheels, and flooded ore pits, he prepared a small booklet on Connecticut's vanished iron industry, which appeared as part of the Connecticut Society of Civil Engineers 51st Annual Report in 1935. Harte had been both a long-time member of the association and also its president. He also authored other carefully-documented works on the state's copper, minor minerals, and the famous Farmington Canal.

In 1940, at the age of ten, I was introduced to Mine Hill's gaunt furnace and especially its excitingly-spooky tunnel system. A dozen years later I returned to Mine Hill in my first car, a 1948 Jeep, whose four-wheel drive was eminently suited to ascend the former ore-car roadbed. In a continuing series of both underground and documentary explorations, I mapped mine tunnels and recorded the Hill's tortuous corporate history.

One reference of great interest was a few photographs of Mine Hill in Harte's iron publication. I regret now, of course, that I did not make an effort to reach him, but probably thought that he had already passed from the scene. But perhaps it was just as well; had I made some contact to satisfy a narrow, if important, technical interest, I might well have then gone my way, leaving his immense collection to eventual dispersion and/or discard.

With the preservation of Mine Hill by the Roxbury Land Trust in 1980, my historical instincts were again awakened, leading to additional on-site and documentary researches. In 1988, a chance attending of a lecture on the famous New Haven and Northampton Canal ("The Farmington") illustrated with photographs taken by Harte, led to contact with his daughter and thence with Mr. Charles R. Harte, Jr., then living in a Chicago suburb. Mr. Harte graciously loaned a set of negatives of Mine Hill, adding immensely to my understanding of the furnace complex. This was soon followed by other mining scene prints and negatives . . . and not a moment too soon . . .

As it turned out, Mr. and Mrs. Harte were preparing to sell their home of some fifty years and move into an Indiana retirement community. With the exception of a relatively small number of family-oriented negatives, the entire collection was up for dispersal or, worse, disposal. Soon, scores of neatly-boxed negative albums (made from classic, black-and-white-mottled cover school composition books) were arriving, later followed by notebooks crammed with handwritten descriptions of iron-making and canal-building activities.

Being an engineer (civil and electrical) by profession, Charles R. Harte kept meticulous documentation of his photographic subjects; each negative bore a serial number (commencing with 0001 on Friday, March 13, 1908, when he arrived in New Haven to take up his new assignment for the New Haven Railroad), the subject, locale, and date. Similar information was written into a series of 4.5-by-7-inch ring-binder notebooks. The last entry, number 22,564, was made on October 14, 1956, of his new twin grandchildren . . . just a month before his death on November 13 at the age of eighty-six. Had his old folding Kodak been examined in time, even later photographs of his last four weeks might have been preserved.

Mortality, however, was not present in Harte's immediate thoughts; the last of his negative notebooks contained blank numbered entries for future photographs going well past the 23,000 mark. And only two days earlier, he had given a lecture to a historical group in Simsbury on his beloved Farmington Canal.

Today, much of his collection has been reasonably preserved. Some materials on the trolley industry were previously donated to the Branford Electric Railway (Shore Line Trolley Museum) and many Farmington Canal negatives repose at the Connecticut Historical Society in Hartford.

Looking back over these recent years, Charles Rufus Harte seems to grow in stature as person, parent, engineering professional, and conscientious historian of a vanished way of life. I would have vastly enjoyed being with him on his various projects, and, as a final accolade, I think he would have made a "great" grandfather, as well . . . !

Frederick W. Chesson
April 1995

Charles Rufus Harte's New Haven

Although Charles Rufus Harte was born in Marietta, Ohio, on November 8, 1870, his roots, like those of many Buckeye State natives, were back east in the Charter Oak's native soil. Indeed, an ancestor, one Captain Rufus Harte, made New Haven his home port, and his mother, Willamena Porter Butler, had long family ties to nearby New London.

When Charles was thirteen years old, he and sister Julia returned to New London, where he graduated from Bulkley High School in 1888. By 1890, when New Haven's burgeoning population passed the 80,000 mark, he was studying Engineering at Columbia University.

After graduating in 1893, Charles soon joined the New Haven Railroad and was first employed as a junior surveyor, cutting brush and driving marker stakes on the right-of-ways. Within five years he had risen to assistant engineer, and in 1899–1900, he had charge of double-tracking the line from Derby north to Union City in Naugatuck.

In 1900, the thirty-year-old Harte temporarily left the New Haven Railroad, whose name-sake city had almost reached a population of 110,000 people, and was by far the state's leading manufacturing and transportation center. Between 1900 and 1904, he was with the firm of Stone and Webster in Boston, where he built interurban electric railways at such diverse locales as Sidney, Nova Scotia, Cape Breton Island, and Terra Haute, Indiana.

On November 14, 1900, he married Helen Louise Wilder of Boston, where daughter Rebekah and son Charles R. Harte, Jr., were born in 1904 and 1907, respectively. In 1908, the New Haven Railroad, which he had rejoined in 1904, required a relocation to New Haven. John Williams was born there that fall, and Virginia in 1910, completing the Harte family. The Census of that year showed a population rise of 25,000 people in the Elm City, and by 1920 it had leaped to what would become a plateau of 162,500 people.

This population surge coincided with the great years of both the New Haven Railroad and its trolley subsidiary, the Connecticut Company. Charles became chief engineer for building new lines, electrifying old steam routes, and the construction of power houses, transmission lines, and car barns. He was involved with trolley lines in the Waterbury-Woodbury and Putnam-Norwich areas, and with the hydro-power station at Bulls Bridge on the Housatonic River. One of his largest projects was the huge, two-level James Street Car Barn, built in 1910, with some 5 miles of track.

During World War I, he was in charge of a War Department project for mapping all electric lines along the East, West, and Gulf Coasts for co-ordinated use by the Army's costal batteries, in case of enemy seaborne attacks.

Much of his time in 1921 was devoted to a rebuilding of the Dyre Dam Power Station, near

Danielson, Connecticut, which he recorded in the form of extensive photographic documentation. One picture shows him in a diving suit, preparing to examine the underwater erosion problems. He also documented the Connecticut Company's many revenue-generating amusement parks: White City, Lighthouse Point, and Momauguin (around New Haven), and Highland Lake (in the Winsted-Torrington Division).

New Haven's growth in the 1920s was mirrored, and then exceeded, by its neighboring towns of East and West Haven, Milford, North Haven, Woodbridge, and Hamden. For the trolley, however, the Roaring Twenties saw an accelerating decline nation-wide, due to the growth of the automobile and a new suburbanite population. The Connecticut Company began to introduce busses for outlying routes and constructed a large garage on Haven Street as early as 1923, as illustrated by Harte's carefully documented photographs. Good times for trolleys and the Elm City ended as the Depression arrived, along with the Census takers, who found the 1930 population virtually unchanged at 162,500.

With its parent forced into receivership in 1935, the Connecticut Company began a crash program of "bus-titution" of trolley lines, commencing with the already marginal lines in eastern Connecticut. Bridgeport was de-railed in 1935, Waterbury in 1937, and Hartford by 1941. Rails were already being uprooted in New Haven and new busses filling up the converted car barns, when an event occurred which gave moribund car lines all over America a new, if temporary, lease on life . . . Pearl Harbor.

During the hectic war years, anything on wheels could find work, and New Haven trolleys which had carried defense workers in 1917 and 1918, carried on from 1941 through 1945. With new busses almost unavailable, the Connecticut Company came up with some strange innovations, such as home-built tractor-trailer combinations which Harte photographed and differentiated as "Catawumpus" and "Kittywumpus" according to relative size.

After the victory over the Axis, the replacement of streetcars was accelerated all over America, with New Haven's ancient open cars hanging on for one unique reason . . . Yale Bowl. Brought out of hibernation from the dusty back storage areas, they could carry literally roof-top loads of football fans out Chapel Street to "The Bowl." But nostalgia could not halt progress, and with the Yale-Connecticut game of September 25, 1948, the last trolleys in the state came to the end of their line.

Harte, however, was active in preserving a portion of this former "Empire of City Rails" and helped found the now thriving Branford Electric Railway Association Museum in East Haven. Here, scores of trolleys from far and wide are not only preserved and restored, but operated for the enjoyment and historical enlightenment of thousands of visitors yearly.

New Haven was the home base, or port, to another form of transportation, now almost totally forgotten, the Farmington-Northampton Canal. Dug from 1825 to 1835 under the most trying conditions, it offered a relatively swift trip for cargo and passengers from New Haven to Northampton, Massachusetts. An express packet boat could make the run in twenty-four hours, with luck. Considering the passage went through sixty locks, the transit time was quite rapid. However, floods, drought, winter closings, and endless maintenance problems finally made the venture a financial failure and much of the towpath was converted to a railbed in 1848 for the new New Haven and Northampton Railroad. In 1933, eighty-five years later, Charles Harte commenced a detailed photographic study of the still-existing locks and waterways, employing both his engineering skills and historical scholarship. Because of his perseverance, this priceless relic of Connecticut's most ambitious, yet little-known, industrial enterprise endures to amaze and inspire.

Another legacy, Connecticut's vanished iron industry, then took Harte's fancy. Existing mostly in the Litchfield County's north-west "Iron Triangle," native iron had helped forge the Colony's will for independence. The charcoal-fueled furnaces carried on stubbornly against the industry's move west and the last blast furnace was not blown out until 1923. Traveling about the back roads of Canann, Kent, Roxbury, and Salisbury, Harte took scores of photographs of abandoned stacks, foundries, and massive water-wheels.

From the recently defunct to the long-dead, Charles Harte turned his old Kodak on Connecticut's tiny and often neglected Colonial-Era grave yards, with their quaint and crumbling head-stones of lurid skulls and smiling cherubs. His excursions extended to much of eastern Massachusetts and other locales in New England, so that his collection could be described as a record of "Yankees in Eternity."

Harte could hardly have said to retired in the formal sense, as he was with the Connecticut Company officially until March 1951. He then continued to visit his dusty office in the old Grand Avenue car barn, there to sort out an Augean Stable of old records which, by law, had to be retained over arbitrary time periods.

In the meantime, he took on new activities, including research of the historic Saugus Iron Works, near Lynn, Massachusetts, now a National Park site. At age eighty, he made frequent trips there to assist with restoration and photographic documentation. He was also active in the preservation of the Eli Terry Waterwheel in Terryville, Connecticut. In addition, every August, for many years, he attended the Columbia Engineering School reunions at Camp Columbia, just south of Bantam Lake in Morris, Connecticut. Even the Great Flood of August 1955 did not deter him and he made valuable photographic records of the disaster's aftermath in several communities. One of his great sorrows was the loss of the famous aqueduct which had once carried the Canal across the Framington River.

He was also a natural history enthusiast and became a specialist on birds, moths, and butterflies. To record his many varied subjects he carefully compiled an indexed film collection of over 22,000 negatives. Both his Farmington Canal and iron industry photographs numbered in the hundreds, as did his careful documentation of the Harte family history and day-to-day activities.

Harte's many memberships included presidency of the American Electric Railway Association and the Connecticut Society of Civil Engineers. He was chairman of the Electrical Standards Committee of the American Standards Association and received its Medal of Recognition on October 24th, 1956, three weeks before his death. He was also president of the Collector's Club of New Haven and the Westville Civic Association and held memberships in the New Haven Colony Historical Society, the Hamden Historical Society, the New York State Historical Society, and the Antiquarian and Landmarks Society.

His papers appearing in the transactions and annual reports of the CSCE began with "The Boston-Providence Railroad Extension" in 1905 and included such diverse works as "The Farmington Canal," "River Obstructions of the Revolutionary War," "Connecticut's Iron Industry," "Connecticut's Minor Metals and Her Minerals," "Connecticut's Cannon," and "Preservation of Beckley Iron Furnace." His last paper, "An Unusual Hydro-Electric Plant Accident and its Repair," appeared in the CSCE 65th Annual Report of March 15, 1948.

He was active to the very end of his long and useful life. In his last year, his interests returned to his original vocation, electric transportation, and he was busy compiling information on the pioneering trolley systems of the inventor Charles Van Depoele, for a new publication.

Charles Rufus Harte died suddenly, on Tuesday, November 13, 1956, at his home of over thirty years in Westville, five days after his eighty-sixth birthday. Just one week previously, he had spoken before the Simsbury Historical Society on his beloved Farmington-Northampton Canal.

References

Charles R. Harte, Jr. Various communications to author.
Connecticut Society of Civil Engineers. Annual Report for 1956: 144-145.
Connecticut Society of Civil Engineers. Various publications of the 1930s.
New Haven Evening Register. 1956. Obituary, November 13: 1.
New Haven Journal-Courier. 1956. Obituary, November 14: 18.
New Haven Sunday Register. 1951. Article, September 2: 5.

One
Old New Haven

Practically from its founding, New Haven was noted for its fine oysters. From wading and shallow-water tonging, the local industry grew until its specialized powered harvesting boats made Fair Haven the "Oyster Capital of New England." Eventually, oysters were transplanted from Chesapeake Bay and allowed to "ripen" in the colder waters of the Sound to yield a superior flavor.

Chapel Street, looking west from Orange (top) and State (bottom) Streets, had almost a frontier look, with gas or oil lamps and hitching rails, when these copies by Harte were originally made in mid-nineteenth century.

Old Chapel Street looking west from Church Street.

State Street, looking west from Parade, also has a western settlement look in this Harte copy.

For many years, the Tontine Hotel, at Church and Court Streets, was a mecca for both Elm City residents and travelers, enduring into the early trolley era. It was famous for its home-grown New Haven oysters.

On July Fourth, 1893, just after Charles Harte had graduated from Columbia University, the Chapel Street Railroad Station burned, destroying architect Henry Austin's Italianate Revival masterpiece.

Taken from a church steeple about the time of the Civil War, this view of Fair Haven includes the covered Railroad Bridge and horse cars on Grand Avenue.

Eli Whitney's cotton gin brought fame to New Haven, but real prosperity came from his Armoury in Whitneyville.

When Harte returned to New Haven in 1908, electric power was still being supplied on a very local basis: witness this maze of wires leaving the New Haven Electric Company's power house at George and Temple Streets. Although trolleys had been in use for some fifteen years, only horse power is visible in this October 31 picture.

Two

Elm City: Family Roots and New Saplings

Harte's mother was Willamena Porter Butler of New London. His father was William S. Hart(e), a merchant of Marietta, Ohio.

Charles' sister, Caroline, was accomplished in the arts. She was for many years a researcher for the Russell Sage Foundation in New York City.

In 1937, Harte returned to his teen-age home of fifty years ago on New London's Meridian Street. Despite being moved and with a store on the ground floor, he thought it little changed.

Just out of Columbia, twenty-four-year-old Charles R. Harte posed by his transit level in a railroad setting that would occupy his entire adult life.

Wisteria-covered Sagamore Cottage was the Harte summer home at Woodmont, an independent Borough of Milford, just over the West Haven line.

The Maternity Wing of New Haven Hospital. Jack and Virginia Harte were born here in November 1908 and August 1910, respectively.

On July Fourth, 1909, five-year-old Rebekah and two-year-old Charles, Jr., examine shell treasures on Woodmont Beach.

During the winter of 1911–1912, the Hartes lived at 141 Center Street in West Haven. The eclectic furnishings included an interesting desk and chair set.

The 1912 Harte Christmas tree featured electric bulbs, powered by batteries in the covered base. Toys included dollies, a Noah's Ark, and a toy village with at least one trolley.

A year later, Helen poses with the family. On the back of the original mounted photograph, their engineer father has diligently recorded the vital records: "Woodmont, November 2, 1913. Rebekah 9 1/2, Charles 6 1/2, Jack 5, Virginia 3 1/4."

The day after the Christmas of 1915, Mr. Harte snapped the family setting out for church or a Sunday visit, the girls clutching their new dolls.

At about this time, Charles posed for a rare formal portrait, dressed in vest, Ascot tie, and high collar.

Charles, Jr., follows in his father's footsteps as a naturalist, butterfly net in one hand, on Mt. Greylock, Massachusetts, August 1915.

Twenty years later, he repeats the pose in the same setting, for the same camera.

Two years later, grand children David, Teddy, and Virginia Anne Clark are off on a butterfly safari in Ossipee, New Hampshire. Same net, same camera . . .

Soaked to the skin from his efforts, cousin Harold Wilder proudly shows off his "first fish" (barely visible below the hand holding the pole) taken on his July 20, 1916, visit to Woodmont.

Charles, Jr., tries his hand at returning a high ball. He went on to play tennis at Yale.

Its bubble-blowing time for Virginia and friend, mid-September, 1916.

New neighbor Alice Young shows off her fancy swivel-top carriage on a late April day in 1916.

Virginia shows off her pet box turtle, who isn't so keen about staying around the kids and cats.

Jack cooking up pancakes on the beach.

Charles and cousin Ed Wilder bring home a mess of skates, causing the family felines to forget their manners.

The Hartes did not let six months of war interfere with life at Woodmont. Here they enjoy a late summer picnic on the beach, roasting hot dogs.

Trying their hand at muskrat trapping, Charles, Jr., and Jack prove that they are indeed "The Two Muskra-teers."

Big sister Rebekah gives her father's camera a rather grumpy look. Maybe its the long black stockings and high-button shoes!

In 1917 Halloween was influenced by the war in Europe as shown by Rebekah's and Virginia's costumes.

The whole family gets into the fun of sliding down the overturned hull of a storm-tossed barge on Woodmont Beach. The late October gale was a harbinger of a bitter winter to follow.

Four kids and four kittens, with one for Mom, made for quite a handful on July 28, 1918.

Jack proves he's a "Good Skate" by bringing home this seven-pounder. It's October 13, and the armistice is only a month away.

Jack and Virginia posed with friends at Woodmont, sporting the styles of the early "Roaring Twenties."

In October 1919, after some ten years in rented quarters, Harte bought his own home at 28 West Elm Street in Westville. It had changed little when he took this snowy view of it on January 15, 1954.

Unable to find the source of a troublesome leak at the Dyre Power Dam up in Danielson, Charles, now fifty years old, braved the icy waters in a diving suit to literally "get to the bottom of things."

Washing young "Lassie" was a family affair on this Saturday in May 1921. The dressed-up attire for father and children was not unusual for these times, when clothing defined "one's place in society."

We leave the Hartes for now with this family group shot taken on June 16, 1929. Charles, Jr., has just graduated from Yale, while Jack has completed his freshman year. Virginia is attending Wellesley, her mother's alma mater, while Rebekah, now a Wellesley grad, is Mrs. Palmer Clarke, and the mother of Louis Clifford (Teddy) Clarke . . .

Three
All Around the Town

New Haven's most prominent office and municipal buildings flanked the east side of the Green on Church Street. Notable were the Chamber of Commerce Building and the Second National Bank Building on Church Street. The latter was also the Connecticut Company's administrative headquarters. Both stood tall and proud when Harte photographed them on a fine May afternoon in 1941.

The corner of busy Church and Chapel was no place to park, even back in March 1931. Harte labeled this photograph of a Fro-Joy Ice Cream truck caught making a delivery to Ligget's Drug Store as a "Parking Violation." If the trolley tracks were being blocked, a hefty fine could be levied.

Trolleys did not venture into this section of State Street, seen looking north from Chapel, on May 6, 1926. It was given over to motor cars, but a lone wagon can be seen near the bank at right.

New Haven Harbor was often the scene of seemingly opposite activities; either it was being dredged out or filled in. With every decade, more and more mud flats and shallows were reclaimed for industrial and transportation needs, as when the former Canal Basin and Long Wharf areas were filled in for bigger railroad yards. Conversely, larger cargo ships, especially oil tankers, required ever deeper channels and berths. The dredge in this December 1913 picture is working the West River estuary region.

Long a familiar landmark on the upper end of East Shore, Koppers Coke Company regularly belched out spectacular, multi-colored clouds from its giant ovens. Its clean-burning coke was considered a "high-class" fuel, when most residences burned anthracite. Blue Coal, which sponsored "The Shadow" radio show on Sunday, was next in line. The nearby Atlantic Refining Company was also a large area employer.

Acme Wire occupied some of the Whitney Armoury buildings in 1912. The area is now the site of the Eli Whitney and A.C. Gilbert Museum.

On a hot mid-July afternoon in 1910, Mr. Harte photographed the Askin Clothing and McCrea Florist stores on Meadow Street, where striped awnings were both a practical and fashionable summer window dress.

Winter was definitely in the air on this slushy January day in 1922 on Chapel Street near the Union League Club. One of the member's autos has taken refuge on the sidewalk, near the gaudy Hyperion Cinema, lest it be carried off on some trolley bumper.

By the mid-1920s New Haven's streets were bustling and often crowded with vehicular traffic. The city's human population was growing slower now, but its automobile population was burgeoning, as this picture from May 6, 1926, well illustrates.

A view from the Wood Building, looking down into Congress Square. According to the bottle-shaped hands on the Ballantine Beer and Ale Clock, it is 10:10 on the morning of May 11, 1940, the same day as Hitler's Blitzkrieg in Europe.

It was a Monday afternoon in May 1932 when Harte snapped these youngsters crossing Livingstone and Canner Streets from Hooker School, just to the left of the picture.

New Haven Hospital grew up along with the Elm City and Yale University, soon becoming indispensable to both. Its original buildings dated back to 1826 and were already hoary when the Harte family came down from Boston in early 1908. About 1915 it became Yale-New Haven Hospital, through its affiliation with the Yale Medical School.

Extending north from Grove Street and bounded by Prospect and Temple is the short but gracious Hillhouse Avenue, named for entrepreneur and canal promoter James Hillhouse. Thanks to Yale University and its benefactors, the grand and sometimes grandiose architectural treasures lining its shaded walks have been largely preserved. Several were designed by Henry Austin, the architect of the Chapel Street Station, New Haven City Hall, and the Grove Cemetery Gate. Charles Harte took these leafy views just about the time that the Class of 1942 was going straight into a post-graduate school called World War II. Yale President Timothy Dwight lived in this elegant Italianate house.

The Skinner House makes another Italianate statement, its tower reminiscent of the former Chapel Street Station.

The already stately Hotchkiss House was framed by massive old elms.

Boardman was another Farmington Canal promoter. His columned portico presented the grace and dignity of a Greek temple.

The rather modest Dana House seems quite dominated by elm and ivy.

The Henry Farnum House suggests a co-mingled English manor and French chateau.

Just around the corner from Hillhouse Avenue is the Colonial Revival home of the New Haven Colony Historical Society, designed by J.F. Kelley and built about 1930. Charles Harte was a long-time member here.

The "Gingerbread Gothic House" at State and Rock Streets.

The Hubinger House on Whalley Avenue was typical of the exuberant Carpenter's Gothic homes of the Elm City's later Victorian architectural period.

Noah Webster's residence on Temple Street was a long-time New Haven landmark when Harte photographed it on July Fourth, 1936. Before long, however, Henry Ford carried it off to his Dearborn Village's historic subdivision in Michigan.

Four
New Haven on the Move

Ever since its founding, coastal and deep-sea shipping had been New Haven's life blood. With the coming of the railroad, this diminished considerably, but sailing ships still carried lumber and coal well into the twentieth century. A three-masted schooner off Woodmont, August 1913.

Paddle-wheel steamers like the *Cepheus*, shown docked at Roton Point, kept regular schedules between New Haven and New London, Providence, and Hartford to the east, and Bridgeport, Norwalk, Stamford, and New York City to the west.

This floating dock served boat passengers where the Mill and Quinnipac Rivers entered New Haven Harbor many years ago.

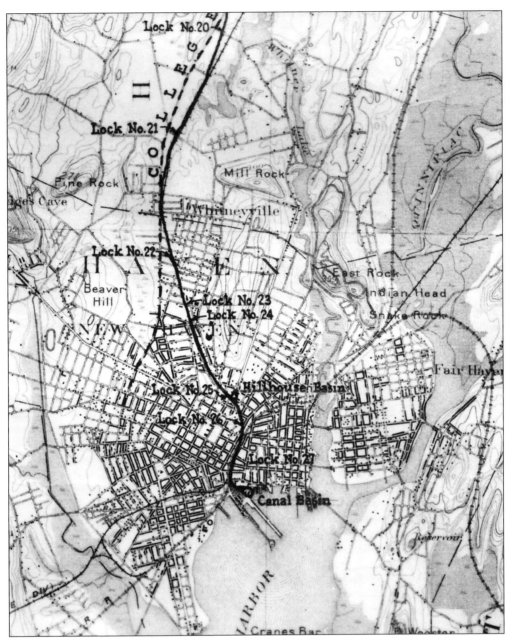

The Farmington Canal started at what is now Brewery Street and made its way north through Cheshire, Plainville, Farmington, Granby, and into Northampton, Massachusetts, transiting sixty locks in its progress. The aqueduct across the Farmington River was Connecticut's greatest engineering feat of the time. Its turbulent active life from about 1830 to 1850 was fraught with natural and financial peril at every lock, so to speak. And when Charles Harte came back to New Haven in 1908, the canal towpath had been given over to the "iron horse" for some sixty years. Twenty-five years later he was to bring it back to life on paper. In 1933 he commenced an exhausting technical and historical survey of the now century-old abandoned canal, mapping and photographing its entire length, from the New Haven Basin up to the Northampton terminus. This map, one of dozens, shows the location of eight New Haven area locks.

Farmington Canal boats were similar to this one in a copied photograph, shown stern-first at a basin. The top-hatted skipper and his wife stand by the impressive tiller.

Canal boats carried both cargo and passengers. The latter were briefly accommodated exclusively in the packet boats described in this 1839 timetable. The newly-built *Doe*, *Fawn*, and *Hart* were "warranted to be furnished in the best manner" and to be under "gentlemanly and obliging commanders, who will spare no pains to promote the comfort of the passengers." The fare from New Haven to Northampton was $3.75 plus "found" or basic food and accommodations. Passage time was an even twenty-four hours, reasonable, considering the necessity of transiting some sixty locks. Unfortunately, patronage was scarce (the fare was a week's wage or more for most workers at this time) and the three "deer" packets were soon sold.

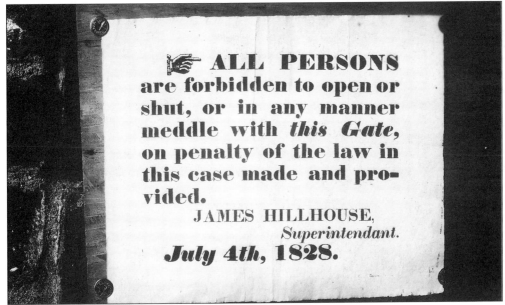

Accidental and intentional mischief were only a few of the many problems besetting the canal's operation. Superintendent Hillhouse felt that July Fourth was an appropriate time to publish this warning on lock-gate "meddling," perhaps implying sanctions by the government.

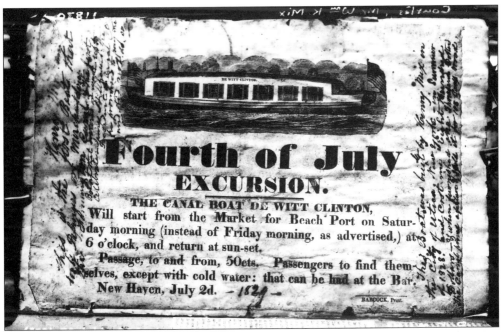

A Fourth of July canal boat excursion was promised by this 1829 poster. The *De Witt Clinton* (named for the Empire State's governor and Erie Canal supporter) would start at a sobering 6 a.m. for Beach Port in Cheshire. Neither fireworks nor firewater were provided in the 50¢ fare, though the latter was available at the on-board bar, along with free cold water for those frugal or abstemious passengers.

NEW HAVEN AND NORTHAMPTON
CANAL
STEAMBOAT LINE.

THE STEAMBOAT
SALEM

Will leave the Belle Wharf and

Canal Basin Wharf, New Haven, for New York, every **MONDAY** and **THURSDAY**, at 9 o'clock **P. M.** Returning, leave Old Slip, New York, every **TUESDAY** and **FRIDAY**, at 4 o'clock **P. M.**

Freight and passengers taken at reduced prices.

For further information, inquire on board, or at **N. A. BACON'S** Store, Canal Basin Wharf, New Haven, or of the Subscribers.

J. & N. BRIGGS, *Agents, No. 40 South St.*
and **F. H. ABBOT**, *No. 52 Wall St. New York.*

The canal company expanded its activities from canal barges to a twice-weekly over-night passenger and freight service to New York on the side-wheeler *Salem*.

When Harte commenced his explorations of the Farmington Canal, only ruins, like this grafitti-daubed wall of Lock 23 near Winchester Avenue, remained. The stone arch at Shepherds Brook in Hamden was still in reasonable condition, after over a century of service, first for the canal and then the railroad.

In its earliest days as a city, New Haveners relied largely upon private transportation. Those who could afford riding horses and carriages maintained their own barns or patronized livery stables, but the vast majority "rode shank's mare" and walked to and from work. Omnibuses, resembling Old West stage coaches, operated out of Fair Haven and Westville in the 1850s, though by the time of the Civil War, horsecars were largely replacing them in urban areas. Typical of the pre-horsecar days was this "Tally-Ho" coach, photographed horseless outside of the Yale Bowl.

Later came the public coach, or omnibus, leading to our present-day "bus." The elegantly-decorated Saltonstall ran through East Haven and into New Haven.

The first streetcars of 1861 brought instant liberation to pedestrians. Working men were no longer tied to tenements near their jobs, and the middle classes could do their shopping with far greater convenience. As new lines extended outward into the then-existing suburbs, a building boom followed and tax bases rose in response. Track laying also resulted in road paving in many areas, adding to both net worth and civic pride. When Charles R. Harte was born in 1870, horse power moved almost every street railway. In New Haven the Fair Haven and Westville line had nearly fifty cars and some three hundred horses at its peak. Equipment was similar to Car No. 73, photographed on Wethersfield Avenue in Hartford around 1880.

When Harte came to work for the New Haven Railroad, all of its locomotives, including this one, were steam powered. When he retired, diesel and electricity were the sole motive-power sources.

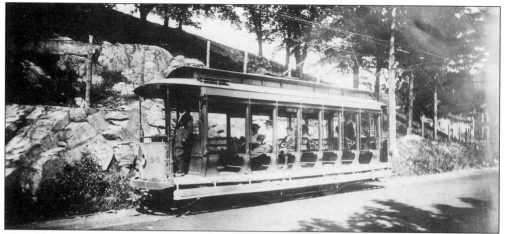

The electric trolley arrived in 1892, much to the relief of residents near the Grand Avenue Horse Barn, whose 350 equines insisted upon both eating and excreting, whether they were out pulling cars or not. Three years later, the transition to electric power was virtually complete, and the Fair Haven & Westville Railroad Company listed eighty electric passenger cars on its 1895 roster, but only "6 Old Horsecars."

By 1900, it had bought up some thirteen rival street railways and was the largest operation in Connecticut, having carried over sixteen million passengers. Its own corporate existence, however, was about to be terminated by an even larger entity, the New Haven Railroad. In May 1904, the company was sold for over ten million dollars and its assets turned over to the New Haven's trolley-operating division, the Consolidated Railroad.

Further transit acquisitions followed, and by 1910 the new Connecticut Company had become the state's principal transit operator. Growth continued up to about the time of World War I, then began a slow but accelerating decline as the automobile gained ascendancy. In less than forty years, the Connecticut Company's streetcar empire was to vanish entirely, the last trolley clattering off into oblivion in New Haven at the dusk of September 25, 1948.

The early single-truck (four wheel) former horsecar pictured here was typical of turn-of-the-century electric streetcars.

The New Haven area was a working laboratory for trolley development. These two Van Depoele cars, with their ungainly poles, ran between Ansonia and Derby c. 1888, about the time Charles Harte entered Columbia University.

Even such tiny stations as Oyster River and Anderson Avenue in Woodmont were tastefully designed, with picket fence-style roof trim.

Emulating their big-brother steam railroads, the larger trolley lines had their own private cars. The pride of the Connecticut Company was No. 500. With its elegant scrolled iron-work platforms and plush interior appointments, it proudly carried company dignitaries to all important functions. Here it poses in North Woodbury on September 1, 1908, for the opening of the line from Waterbury, which was engineered by Charles Harte.

Car 500's interior boasted green-plush cushions on wicker armchairs for the traveling dignitaries, with a galley and lavatory for their creature comforts.

Besides passengers, the Connecticut Company also carried light freight and parcels in a fleet of trolley express cars. Early morning runs specialized in milk cans from dairy farms as far away as Woodbury.

Horse-drawn wagons usually came out second best when disputing the right-of-way of trolleys .

As a civil engineer, Harte was instrumental in building the Connecticut Company's largest car barn, on James Street. The parent New Haven Railroad's main line in the foreground is not yet electrified

Harte was persuaded to take a moment from his busy engineering duties to pose at his office desk, briefcase ready at hand, on September 30, 1916.

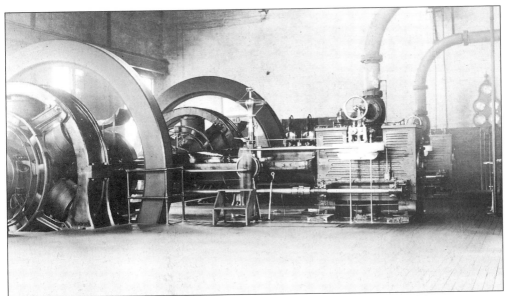

Trolleys required some 600 volts of direct current, which was mainly supplied from generators driven by massive steam engines or the newer turbines.

Supplying large amounts of direct current power to fleets of trolleys required miles of very heavy and expensive feeder cables. This ten-line distribution network for the Manufacturers' Railroad radiated out from Power Station A, near Humphrey Street. The normal vulnerability of such a system to ice storms and other natural disasters was heightened by fears of German sabotage in August 1917, when this picture was taken.

Trolleys and buses line up at Union Station for football patrons. Big football games, such as the November 13, 1937, Yale-Princeton encounter, brought scores of trolleys and busses to the New Haven Railroad Station to transport the hordes of fans to and from the Bowl.

Ancient open cars were kept on hand for one reason alone . . . Yale Bowl. Here, Car No. 1448 loads up with football fans on the day of the big game.

The old New Haven Station is seen c. 1915. Motor cars are conspicuous by their near-total absence.

By 1920, most of the Connecticut Company's far-flung trolley lines were well-established, and construction activities were now mainly of a maintenance nature. The system's infrastructure—roadbed, rails, cars, overhead, and power plant—required endless attention, lest a failure in any link cause an entire line to collapse. Track repair was infrequent but demanding. Rails could be cut by acetylene torch, but welding required use of a virtual incendiary bomb, called Thermite, composed of aluminum grit and iron oxide. When ignited, the aluminum became oxidized and the rust returned to molten iron, welding the rail segments. Streetcars, by their very nature, were designed for a long, nitty-gritty, street existence. The Connecticut Company's chief suppliers, Wason, Brill and Osgood Bradley, built their cars to last. When service ended in New Haven in September 1948, some of the rolling stock had seen forty years of duty, including two World Wars. And a few lucky survivors, now at several scattered trolley museums, are still loyally carrying visitors, some fifty years later!

Car No. 3211's damage demonstrates the consequences on a typical trolley-auto confrontation, one of the perils of limited maneuverability. While on the Church-Chapel Street run, it had its headlight and Yale-Harvard baseball sign bashed in.

Repairs to the network of over-head trolley and feeder cables were both costly and time-consuming. Routine wire repair and replacement had to be done in off-peak hours, lest revenue-producing schedules be upset. For this work, electric and self-propelled tower cars were used. For more urgent and emergency repairs, gas-powered tower trucks were deployed.

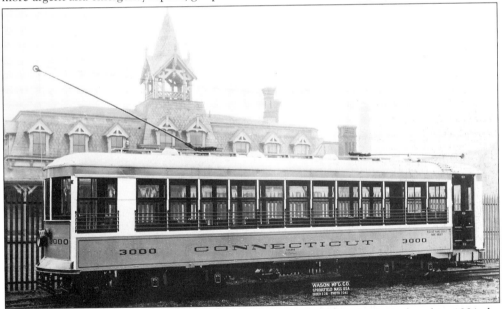

In an effort to pare ever-mounting costs, the Connecticut Company introduced in 1921 the light-weight, one-man operated Birney "safety car." Included was a "dead man's switch" to halt the car automatically, should the motorman faint or even drop dead at his post. The ultra-light, four-wheel versions were little bigger than some horsecars. They proved to be poor riders, prone to derailing, and were replaced by double-truck cars, like No. 3000. Around 1920, this double-truck Birney safety car proudly posed for its builder's picture at the Wason Company. Unlike so many of its contemporaries, you can still ride on No. 3000, at the Shore Line Trolley Museum in East Haven.

Car No. 500 continued to uphold its prestige. Officials of the Public Utilities Commission made their annual inspections of the state's steadily-shrinking lines in its relative comfort. This group of PUC and Connecticut Company officials posed by the veteran car on July 15, 1934, as the end of the line neared for Derby trolley riders. Old 500 is now the pride of the trolley museum and still carries special visitors from East Haven out to Short Beach.

This Mack diesel Bus No. 1029 crossing the Grand Avenue Bridge in February 1947 was a harbinger of the end of the trolley era in New Haven.

Instead of repairing the overhead, the tower truck was now cutting it down for salvage, as at Granniss Corner, East Haven, in March 1947. Breaking the adjacent paving was the first step to recovering old track for scrap. Next would come an "up-rooter" for extracting the rails. The appearance of these ominous vehicles literally meant "end of the line" for the abandoned trolley route.

"Don't Be A Road Hog" this 1929 sign in Westville urged motorists, but accidents were bound to happen anyway.

This Model T pickup truck met its Waterloo in the form of an East Haven telephone pole on July 13, 1923. And, yes, it WAS Friday the 13th!

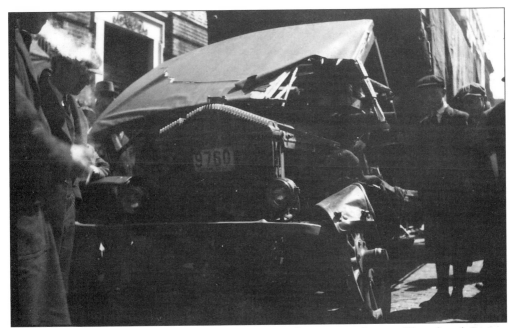

This otherwise sturdy-looking vehicle seems to have been stepped on at Chapel and Orange Streets, perhaps done in by an immovable trolley.

Another auto came to grief at the corner of Green and Wallace Streets.

Unlike the tried and true trolleys, the new busses were prone to breakdowns, especially from flat tires and motor troubles. This "emergency station" at 210 Meadow Street was set up to send out repair vehicles. Next door, the Volk Hotel offered rooms for $1, while farther down was the Arlington at 152 Meadow Street.

By 1926 busses had become large and substantial enough to offer trolleys serious competition, as is apparent in this scene at Orange and Chapel Streets.

Complete with curtained windows, new Bus No. 177 sets off for Bridgeport, carrying former trolley patrons, April 1931.

New buses for New Haven.

Mr. Harte's sedan is on a Weaver Auto Hoist at this Westville gas station, which offered a "greasing & spraying" service for $1.50, in August 1929.

By the mid-1930s, gas stations had sprung up on street corners all over the city. Most were owned or franchised by the big oil companies, like this Socony Station on Congress and Washington Avenues. The Flying Red Horse was a familiar sight to motorists, along with the sign for Firestone Tires

Five
New Haven at Play

Woodmont's 1916 Decoration Day (now Memorial Day) parade included a nursing-detachment, with their young but alert patient.

Savin Rock, with its beaches, restaurants, rides, and entertainments, was a mecca for visitors from as far away as Waterbury. The Connecticut Company not only brought patrons directly there, but built their own resort, the White City, as a park within the park. Harte was involved with its maintenance and took many photographs during its hey-day in the twenties. Lereve's Park Lunch was a favorite spot for refreshment, set among rows of Savin Rock's graceful arching elm trees, as on this early June day in 1923.

The band stand at Savin Rock was a popular spot for quiet enjoyment.

Madam Annette (Polska Wruszka) promised to "Reveal All" from a mere glance at your palm, according to this sign outside her striped tent.

For more excitement, a visit to the Old Mill Fun House was in order. But all is quiet on this early October day of 1923, and the park is closed for the season . . .

The Woodmont summer community climaxed its season with a water carnival, held at the harbor jetty in late August, 1911.

Bathers at Lighthouse Point Beach may have found this August day in 1918 on the chilly side from the off-shore breeze.

In a respite from the stresses of World War I on the home front, New Haveners could relax at the Connecticut Company's Momauguin Beach resort.

A quiet Tuesday afternoon in early June, 1922, found a few hardy souls testing the Sound's chilly waters.

For those who preferred greater solitude, there were bucolic campsites on Kelsey Island off of Short Beach. For others, year-round cottages with full amenities were available.

For Hamden's July Fourth parade, these Legionairs entered a float honoring the Farmington Canal and posed for Harte's camera in 1936.

On May 23, 1954, area Boy Scouts set up their tents for a camporee in Westville Park.

Connecticut Company employees enjoyed such benefits as excursions, sport teams, and an annual outing. This one, held at Lighthouse Point on August 10, 1923, included a foot race, a rolling pin throwing contest, and, of course, a big clam-bake.

The Connecticut Company's 1929–1930 bowling team proudly displays their league trophy.

A mid-1930s happy group is all set to leave on a Company excursion.

Even Company executives were not above hamming it up at this Westport outing in 1938.

For a Halloween parade in October 1946, the Connecticut Company sponsored this attractive float honoring the United Nations.

Even from down on Temple Street, the New Haven Green's Christmas lighting was quite apparent as 1929 was ending.

The first full year of the Depression was ushered out on the New Haven Green with sober hopes for 1931.

New Haven Green aglow with the lights of its tree and adjoining office buildings with specially-lighted windows to usher in the Christmas of 1939.

The "Tree of Light" was a long-time tradition in Westville's community Christmas display.

On Christmas Eve, 1940, a Connecticut Company Santa was on hand to greet adults and kids on Chapel Street.

Six
The Yale Scene

As a graduate of Columbia University, Charles Harte was a both fellow Ivy Leaguer to the Yale community and the father of two of its alumni; Charles, Jr., Class of 1929, and John Williams (Jack) Class of 1932. In the course of his half-century in New Haven, he saw major construction projects transform the once-compact old campus into a sprawling, multi-collegiate institution.

Built between 1917 and 1922, the Harkness Memorial Tower long dominated all other Yale buildings, and many city structures as well. Here, it towers over the newly-leafed elm trees in June 1940.

"God and Man at Yale . . ." are met together in this July 1955 glimpse through lush elms of the Divinity School Chapel.

Strathcona Hall's tower rivals Harkness in this March 1942 setting.

Ivy traces over a windowless wall of the Brazelius Secret Society at Whitney Avenue and Trumbull Street. Founded in 1848, it is junior only to Skull and Bones (1833) and Scoll and Key (1842).

Within the heart of the Old Campus lay Connecticut Hall, Yale's oldest building, photographed for last time by Charles Harte in May 1956.

Yale grads from the Class of 1930 might recall this scene at the intersection of York and Elm Streets during commencement on June 4, 1930.

By 1930, private automobiles were challenging trolleys downtown, as can be seen here at the intersection of College and Chapel Streets. This photograph, like the preceeding one, was taken on June 4, 1930.

Ancient open-cars, such as No. 660 and No. 744, were kept on hand for one reason alone . . . Yale Bowl. Here, on November 13, 1942, they await the onrushing crowds of football fans the following day who will engulf them, filling seats, running boards, and even the commodious flat roof, happily indifferent to the 600-volt-charged trolley pole and overhead wires. As the procession made its way up Chapel Street and on out Derby Avenue to the Bowl, children would scramble for small change thrown by the riders, perhaps as good luck tokens.

A football game at the Bowl.

The Walter Camp Memorial Gate at Yale Bowl.

For a few hours, the ancient cars rested up for the return run back to downtown New Haven. At the game's conclusion, there would be a mad scramble through the classic portals of the Walter Camp Memorial Gate to get a seat, or even a foothold on the roof. Fare collecting under such sardine-can conditions was difficult, at best. This great tradition, going back some fifty years, ended with the Yale-Connecticut game on September 25, 1948, which coincided with the last trolley run in New Haven, and Connecticut, for that matter.

Finally, night descends upon the Yale campus, with the illuminated Harkness Tower standing like a sentinel over all, sending forth its own "Lux et Veritas" to New Haven and the world.

Seven

Meeting the Test

Early New Haven had its share of perils, from plagues and unfriendly Indians to the rival Dutch colony of New Netherlands. When New Amsterdam became New York in 1664, English hegemony assured a century of relative safety, but by 1770, parent-colony relations were becoming strained, as America moved inexorably towards self-rule. In July 1779, British General William Tryon proposed to celebrate the Yankee's third year of independence with a fireworks display composed of New Haven, itself. However, the approach of strong militia forces saved both "town and gown" from immolation. During the War of 1812 New Haven suffered mightily, and the city did not revive economically until the opening of the Farmington Canal and especially the coming of the railroads. Later conflicts brought "alarums of war" to New Haven, but the onus fell mainly upon its volunteers and conscripts. In between were floods, fires, blizzards, and epidemics, plus financial panics, depressions, and their resultant social and economic upheavals. Yet New Haven shouldered on . . . Meeting the Test . . .

This photograph is of the (in)famous blizzard of March 1888, which left New Haven under 50 inches of gale-drifted snow. All wheeled traffic was paralyzed for days, including this stranded Fair Haven and Westville Railway horsecar.

On Washington's Birthday, 1934, Connecticut was hit by a storm rivaling the Blizzard of '88. "It's up to here!" this motorman seems to be saying, indicating the height of a just-plowed snow drift on the Airport Road in West Haven.

Even four days after the storm, Broadway appeared completely deserted on this normally bustling Tuesday afternoon.

A 4-horsepower road grader was brought in to help clear the New Haven Green.

A trolley edges down Portsea Street at Liberty in the grimy aftermath of the storm.

Early fire companies were mostly volunteer manned, with only the horses and driver on full-time call. Some were organized by insurance companies, who placed their "fire marks" on protected buildings so that time, man power, and water would not be wasted on non-clients' burning property.

In this c. 1880 picture, copied by Harte, the local boys seem to have the edge on the apparatus as all race down Artizan Street. It is said that the picture was posed, the boys being given a head start on the horses.

A year after returning to the Elm City, Harte caught this scene as two men fled a fire at "Richard's Place."

A blaze in mid-January 1912 gutted the Sheldon Building and left it an ice-festooned shell.

Smoke billows over downtown from a blaze at Bullard's Department Store in January 1923.

Christmas Eve of 1943 found the corner of Broadway and York an ice-covered shambles of gutted buildings, which also halted trolley movement on Broadway. Notice the tilted sign of the "College Toasty" restaurant on York Street. Was an overheated toaster the cause of it all?

A downpour on August 1, 1927, created instant water hazards for motorists on the way to Savin Rock. Some vehicles were luckier than others . . .

Although the Great Hurricane of 1938 vented its main fury in the Providence area, the entire Connecticut coastline was savaged: hundreds of lives were lost and there was enormous property damage. Entire trolley lines were knocked out through downed wires and washed-out roadbeds, and some marginal ones were never to be restored. The Harte home on West Elm Street escaped serious damage, but other parts of Westville, like Alden Avenue, were battered by fallen trees and power poles.

The Depression was felt keenly all over New Haven, where many once-solid firms were driven into bankruptcy and closure or into limited operations with greatly slashed staffs. The New Haven Railroad itself, parent of the Connecticut Company, was forced into receivership, further curtailing trolley services. The crisis is reflected in this scene at Orange and Elm Street, on a grim February day in 1935.

The human cost of the Depression was profound, with long-term social repercussions. In May of 1930, its effects were already being felt.

When the Harte family came to New Haven in 1908, America had been at peace for some ten years, and only the Balkans rumbled and sputtered in revolt against the moribund Ottoman Empire. But soon the eruption's fall-out engulfed all of Europe, and in April 1917 the Hartes prepared for war on the home front.

By early 1915 New Haveners were quite aware of the war in Europe, as orders for munitions flooded into Winchester and other producers of military goods. On March 29, Harte snapped this "British Air Raid Warning" poster in a local book store window. "Aero-planes" were still on the puny side, but bomb-laden German Zeppelins were regarded with apprehension over here, after raiding London.

The war still seemed remote on July Fourth, 1917, in Woodmont, but the Harte family, plus a few friends, were ready to demonstrate their readiness with a parade of little doughboys and nurses. Armed with everything from wooden guns and swords to a bayonet-mounted air-rifle, they are almost ready to march off, mostly in step, to save Woodmont from the Hun.

One of the local war industries was this concrete barge plant in West Haven.

Helen Harte was a marcher in this parade of Red Cross Volunteers down Church Street on May 18, 1918.

Having learned semaphore signaling as part of her Girl Scout troop's war preparedness program, Rebekah Harte demonstrates her skills by making the letter "G" in this photograph from May 20, 1918.

To help foster cooperation among the Allies, this mass ethnic folk dance was held on the New Haven Green on August 21. Harte climbed to a high vantage point above the Connecticut Company's offices at 129 Church Street to make the shot.

On a murky November 23, 1918, Harte again ventured to a high vantage point to record New Haven's official victory celebration. The central theme was an inflated but grounded artillery observation balloon, a favorite target of the late Red Baron.

War came again from Europe, slowly at first, then with the thunder of Pearl Harbor in December 1941. Soon barrage balloons rose over the strategic waterfront area, while darkness descended upon dimmed out streets and buildings.

World War II came close to the Harte family with the enlistment of Jack in the Army Air Corps. Here he is at home on furlough in July 1943, posing for his father's camera, with an earlier portrait on the bookcase behind him.

Eight

New Haven at Rest

Founded as a strict Puritan theocracy, New Haven was long regarded as a citadel of restrictive and punitive "Blue Laws," minutely regulating both public and private morals and behavior. With the secularizing effects of inter-colonial commerce and the growth of Yale College into a university, the Elm City became more mainstream. Still, the churches on the Green were to set a definitive tone for the place, first in its original Congregational sense, then Episcopal and General Protestant, and finally, in Harte's lifetime, a largely ecumenical community with diverse houses of worship.

Henry Austin's monumental gate of the Grove Street Cemetery. Emerging from a February 1923 snowstorm, it resembles a dune-surrounded Egyptian monument of antiquity, as it proclaims: "The Dead Shall Be Raised."

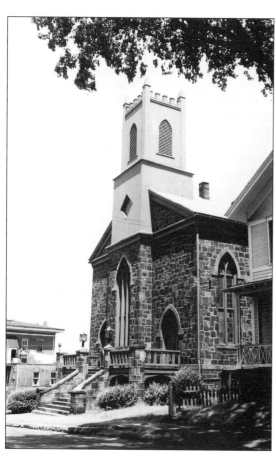

Two stone churches, one on Grand Avenue; the other, incongruously framed by a trio of gas pumps in 1947, in East Haven.

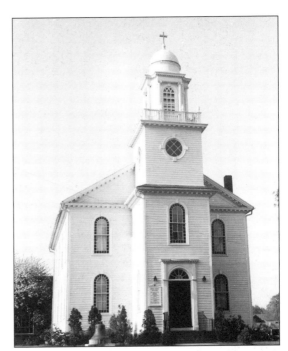

In 1950, Grance Episcopal Church in Hamden had the bell from a former belfry on its front lawn.

Photographed just before Thanksgiving of 1929, Milford's Congregational Church is reflected with great clarity in the old town mill-pond.

This Congregational Church in Madison shows an architectural affinity for its sister parish in Milford.

The purity of line and simple elegance of the Center Church has both dominated and enhanced New Haven Green for over two centuries.

Within Grove Cemetery's crowded acres lie the bodies of the once-renowned and the forever obscure, now all equal in "Skull and Cross-bones Land." Among the many notable monuments is the Trowbridge Memorial, erected in 1930.

Among the older graves is the Morse family stone, which includes three children, a memorial for an entire family of "Yankees in Eternity."

Is this a smiling or a smirking winged face, presiding over the heart-shaped inscription of Deacon Punderson?

East Haven Cemetery has this Bradley family stone for young Uriel and three sets of twin siblings. Certainly a case of "Little Yankees in Eternity."

Nine
The Golden Years

At age sixty-eight, when most men have retired or passed on, Charles Rufus Harte was still hale and active in many pursuits, when given a service award at a March 16, 1939, Engineering Society ceremony.

Two years later, he donned overalls and braved dust and vermin to sort out literally tons of Connecticut Company records for discard or preservation.

In December 1953, Charles R. Harte joined with six other very senior alumni of the Columbia School of Mines Class of 1893 for what was probably their final reunion.

Harte's interest in natural history included birds and butterflies. In this February 1954 home scene, "Andy" the cat poses before a few of the many display frames of moths and butterflies collected over the years.

Even at age eighty-four, Harte kept busy and active with both creative and research projects. Shown in this picture is his hand-crafted tall clock, in this case, a great-grandfather's grandfather clock.

Harte continued to visit the restoration of the historic Saugus Iron Works in Lynn, Massachusetts, and his cousins in Medway through the autumn of 1956. He was busy researching the pioneering electric cars of Charles Van Depoele and was preparing another technical paper at his eighty-sixth birthday on November 8, 1956. He died suddenly, three days later, having just delivered a talk on the Farmington Canal . . . his favorite connection with old New Haven, and its now-vanished world . . .

Ten

A Sense of Place

Each community, town, or region has a unique identity, definable in time and place. Economic and political definitions are often arbitrary and ephemeral, as with the changing seasons. Yet there are certitudes in the lives of those who lived and worked within that entity, no matter how circumscribed; a distinct sense of place, that is both partaken of and generated . . . an essence without which our lives can be ineffably poorer in the long run of things. New Haven was and is so varied a locale in a many-facetted state, that no one image or description could define its essence. Hence, the following images have been chosen in an attempt to show not only what has vanished, but what intangible qualities yet remain to hopefully inspire future generations.

In the above photograph, Sleeping Giant lies in repose, reflected in Clarke's Pond.

This view of enduring East Rock, reflected in the Mill River, was Charles Harte's last photograph of an essential New Haven landmark.

This view northwest from East Rock gives an almost rural view of the New Haven in 1956, perhaps not too much changed from when Harte might have glimpsed it some fifty years earlier.

A view of towering East Rock and the Orange Street Bridge over the Mill River, on a July day in 1940.

A quiet low tide and a restful sunset at the end of the day at Momauguin.

Time stands still at 10:10 on a jeweler's clock at Church and George Streets, with its image of open trolleys, straw hats, and striped awnings on a warm August day in 1922.

Emerging from a wintery gloom, the illuminated Harkness Memorial Tower rises out of a December night in 1950.

Quiet reflections in the West River, as it flows through Edgewood Park in mid-October, 1929, and late August, 1930.

Gone forever are Connecticut's one-room schools, like this one in Woodmont which the Harte children might have attended in 1918.

An autumn storm brings up the surf on a deserted Woodmont beach in October 1908.

Tranquil snow scenes in West Rock Park were favorites of Harte's.

After a wet snow storm early in 1923, only the sounds of singing wires from a distant trolley seem to break the Sunday silence on Edgewood Avenue. Were it not for the overhead wires, one could be back in pre-electric horsecar days.

Never more will the Farmington Canal echo to the boatman's call, nor the locomotive's plaintive whistle, as on this wintry January day in 1933 . . .

A serene view of Broadway, on the last Friday in August 1939. Remember it well, because in just seven days, the world would again be at war, this time for six long years. And nothing would ever be the same . . . either for New Haven, or us all . . .

Acknowledgments

Some of the photographs which appear in this book were copy photographs taken by Charles Rufus Harte from original photographs in the collection of the New Haven Colony Historical Society. I would like to thank the New Haven Colony Historical Society for their kind assistance.

To Charles Rufus Harte, Jr., for graciously furnishing his father's photographic archives and other historical materials and for detailed supportive information over the years. Also, to Virginia Harte Hulbert for valuable background details.

To John Pawloski and Erwin Cohen for valuable photographic services in preparing ancient negatives for state-of-the-art scanning techniques.

To Thomas Sokira for technical and historical information on New Haven and its vanished trolley system.